CLASSIC ROCK FOR TWO

2   Bang a Gong (Get It On)

4   Can't Fight This Feeling

6   Carry on Wayward Son

8   Cold as Ice

10   Come On Eileen

12   Come Together

14   Crocodile Rock

16   Down on the Corner

18   Every Little Thing She Does Is Magic

20   Free Fallin'

22   Hurts So Good

24   The Joker

26   Livin' on a Prayer

    Maggie May

    Mr. Roboto

32   Money for Nothing

34   One More Night

36   Peace of Mind

38   Reeling in the Years

40   Smoke on the Water

42   Summer of '69

44   Uptown Girl

46   You're the Inspiration

Arrangements by Peter Deneff

ISBN 978-1-5400-6540-7

Hal•Leonard®

Visit Hal Leonard Online at
www.halleonard.com

Contact Us:
Hal Leonard
7777 West Bluemound Road
Milwaukee, WI 53213
Email: info@halleonard.com

In Europe contact:
Hal Leonard Europe Limited
42 Wigmore Street
Marylebone, London, W1U 2RN
Email: info@halleonardeurope.com

In Australia contact:
Hal Leonard Australia Pty. Ltd.
4 Lentara Court
Cheltenham, Victoria, 3192 Australia
Email: info@halleonard.com.au

BANG A GONG
(Get It On)

FLUTES

Words and Music by
MARC BOLAN

CAN'T FIGHT THIS FEELING

FLUTES

Words and Music by
KEVIN CRONIN

CARRY ON WAYWARD SON

FLUTES

Words and Music by
KERRY LIVGREN

COLD AS ICE

FLUTES

Words and Music by MICK JONES
and LOU GRAMM

COME ON EILEEN

FLUTES

Words and Music by KEVIN ROWLAND,
JAMES PATTERSON and KEVIN ADAMS

COME TOGETHER

FLUTES

Words and Music by JOHN LENNON
and PAUL McCARTNEY

CROCODILE ROCK

FLUTES

Words and Music by ELTON JOHN
and BERNIE TAUPIN

DOWN ON THE CORNER

FLUTES

Words and Music by
JOHN FOGERTY

EVERY LITTLE THING SHE DOES IS MAGIC

FLUTES

Words and Music by
STING

FREE FALLIN'

FLUTES

Words and Music by TOM PETTY
and JEFF LYNNE

Medium Rock

HURTS SO GOOD

FLUTES

Words and Music by JOHN MELLENCAMP
and GEORGE GREEN

THE JOKER

FLUTES

Words and Music by STEVE MILLER,
EDDIE CURTIS and AHMET ERTEGUN

LIVIN' ON A PRAYER

FLUTES

Words and Music by JON BON JOVI,
DESMOND CHILD and RICHIE SAMBORA

MAGGIE MAY

FLUTES

Words and Music by ROD STEWART
and MARTIN QUITTENTON

MR. ROBOTO

FLUTES

Words and Music by
DENNIS DeYOUNG

Play 3 times

MONEY FOR NOTHING

FLUTES

Words and Music by MARK KNOPFLER
and STING

ONE MORE NIGHT

FLUTES

Words and Music by
PHIL COLLINS

Moderate Ballad

PEACE OF MIND

FLUTES

Words and Music by
TOM SCHOLZ

REELING IN THE YEARS

FLUTES

Words and Music by WALTER BECKER
and DONALD FAGEN

SMOKE ON THE WATER

FLUTES

Words and Music by RITCHIE BLACKMORE,
IAN GILLAN, ROGER GLOVER,
JON LORD and IAN PAICE

SUMMER OF '69

FLUTES

Words and Music by BRYAN ADAMS
and JIM VALLANCE

UPTOWN GIRL

FLUTES

Words and Music by
BILLY JOEL

YOU'RE THE INSPIRATION

FLUTES

Words and Music by PETER CETERA
and DAVID FOSTER